questions: what is the connection between banks and price declines? May bank failures and deflation naturally occur together? Can monetary policy help prevent banking failures, or does deposit insurance suffice? This paper provides answers to these questions.

Economists have long regarded disruptions in the financial sector as a source of economic fluctuations ([19], [2], [4]). The key mechanism works through an increase in the cost of intermediation during a financial crisis: the increased cost causes a decline in credit, which can ultimately lead to periods of low growth and recession. One explanation for the observed protracted decline in output during a financial crisis is that small shocks may be amplified and propagated throughout the financial system and the rest of the economy: this paper provides one such explanation. It describes a novel amplification mechanism of banking crisis and analyzes policy responses that can prevent such amplification from being triggered.

In the model, bank failures are amplified by deflation and at the same time feed back deflation, in a vicious circle[4]. A key friction is that repayments on deposits are fixed in nominal terms, rather than contingent on the realization of prices. Because of this, banks face a mismatch in their balance sheets between the value of their assets (productive projects in which they invest, and loans to firms) and liabilities (deposits). Deposits are at book value because they are indexed to the price level at the time the liability originated, that is, when the deposit contract was signed. Banks' productive projects are valued at current market prices. If prices unexpectedly fall, then the real value of existing nominal obligations increases, but the real value of assets is unchanged[5]: when the decline in prices is large enough, it leads banks to fail (figure 1, right-hand side). When banks fail, depositors drastically reduce deposit holdings and increase cash holdings: a banking panic occurs[6].

The other key and novel ingredient in the model is that banks provide financial intermediation to households by issuing liabilities that can be used as means of payment

---

[4]Deflation is not a necessary condition for the amplification mechanism described in the model: banking crisis may be amplified even by an inflation rate lower than anticipated.

[5]This is equivalent to banks making nominal loans to firms. When the price level falls, firms default on their loans because the real value of their nominal liabilities increases, but the real value of assets (output from productive projects) is unchanged. Therefore when firms default on their loans, banks' assets are just the collateral on the loans, valued at current prices.

[6]Contrary to the mechanism at work in Diamond and Dybvig [15] models, the reason banks fail in this model is not a combination of a coordination failure on the side of depositors and a maturity mismatch in banks' balance sheets. In this model a banking panic occurs when depositors who hold maturing claims at the bank are not paid and do not renew their deposits. The panic is precipitated because depositors expect banks to fail and because banks face a mismatch between nominal liabilities and real assets rather than a maturity mismatch.

alternative to cash (e.g. check and debit card[7]). If banks fail, then the payment instruments they issued are no longer viable to settle transactions. Financial intermediation provided by banks disappears, and cash becomes the only means of payment available to households to purchase consumption goods. Therefore, during a banking crisis, the set of goods that must be paid by cash expands, which causes households' demand for cash to increase. Unless the supply of cash increases, however, the economy will now have too little cash chasing too many consumption goods, and as a consequence prices fall (figure 1, left-hand side). Finally, with deposits falling, banks' investment into productive projects decreases and economic activity declines.

By formalizing such a vicious circle, this paper analyzes policy responses that can prevent the amplification mechanism from being triggered. An active monetary policy prevents prices from falling and banks from failing; as a consequence, economic activity does not decline. Deposit insurance also prevents banks from failing by guaranteeing banks' liabilities. However, if not coupled with strict regulations, it induces moral hazard on the part of banks, which results in larger business cycle fluctuations relative to a monetary policy aimed at keeping prices constant, and it may also result in triggering the amplification mechanism of bank failures as explained later.

The main features of the model in this paper and of the potential policy responses, capture the main aspects of the banking crises that occurred in the United States before the adoption of federal deposit insurance in 1934. Those banking crises took place in an environment with drastic declines in prices and production and were accompanied by a very large increase in the aggregate demand for liquidity. Furthermore, currency usage grew substantially and tended to replace checks as a means of payment[8]. Some of these aspects are common to more recent experiences as well, such as Japan in the 1990s and the recent financial crisis in the United States,[9] thus suggesting that a similar amplification mechanism may have been at work.

This model also formalizes some explanations for the severity of the Great Depression

---

[7]In the model checks and any payment cards are equivalent, to the extent that cards allow households to pay for consumption goods without having to carry cash.

[8]Empirical evidence is reported in appendix A.1. Evidence that bank failures were associated with price declines is consistent with the mechanism that in the model causes banks to default through deflation. Evidence that cash tended to replace checks is consistent with the mechanism that in the model feeds back from bank failures to deflation, working through a reduction in the financial intermediation provided by banks.

[9]For the 2007-2009 financial crisis in the United States, appendix A.3 reports data on currency holdings outside of banks, which increased exactly when prices started falling and large banks failing.

3

and provides support for some policy recommendations that followed it. Irving Fisher's [18] debt-deflation theory of the Great Depression identifies the unanticipated fall in the price level and consequent increase in the real amount of debt as the cause of the depression continuing in a vicious spiral. Fisher's theory also identifies a policy response: reflating the price level up to the average level at which outstanding debts were contracted and maintaining that level unchanged[10].

Friedman and Schwartz [19] and Warburton [27], [28], [29] share a similar view of the role of monetary policy in relieving the severity of the contraction. Friedman and Schwartz [19] see the banking and liquidity crisis as responsible for the decline in the stock of money which, in turn, caused prices to fall[11] and eventually led to the collapse of the banking system. They hypothesize that prevention or moderation of the decline in the stock of money would have reduced the contraction's severity and its duration.

This paper formalizes Friedman and Schwartz's [19] hypothesis: monetary intervention plays a useful role by adjusting the supply of liquidity to prevent prices from falling. This paper also evaluates Friedman and Schwartz's hypothesis relative to deposit insurance, which was established at the federal level in the United States as a response to the failure of monetary authorities to avoid the collapse of the banking system during the early 1930s[12]. It is particularly relevant to this model that deposit insurance causes larger business cycle fluctuations than a monetary policy à la Friedman and Schwartz, because the fluctuations may trigger the amplification mechanism of banking failures described above. Larger output fluctuations cause banks to fail more often, in bad states of the world. If it is not feasible for deposit insurance to guarantee that payments made by checks and cards issued by failed banks are honored in every state of the world, then bank failures cause a reduction in banks' provision of payment services and an increase in the demand for cash, which results in a fall in prices. The vicious circle of banking failures and deflation is thus triggered.

It is crucial in this model that the amplification mechanism of the banking crisis works exclusively through the unanticipated fall in prices: once that is prevented no amplification is triggered. This has important implications for policy because in most banking-panic models[13] a panic is the outcome of a coordination failure among depositors: fearing that

---

[10]Fisher [18], pg. 346

[11]Friedman and Schwartz (pp.351) argue that the failures were the mechanism through which a drastic decline was produced in the stock of money. Absent any policy intervention, prices fell.

[12]See Friedman and Schwartz [19] pp.300−, 420−.

[13]This is a large literature that follows Diamond and Dybvig [15]; among many [17], [24].

other depositors' withdrawals will cause the bank to become insolvent, depositors with no urge to consume (patient depositors) run on the bank. In this paper, no coordination failure among depositors occurs, and therefore deposit insurance has no purpose in guaranteeing sufficient assets at the bank to cover withdrawals by patient depositors and avoid a panic. In this paper, anything that causes a reduction in the financial intermediation provided by banks will induce a fall in prices, which, in turn, puts pressure on the balance sheets of banks that had survived, causing them to fail, so the economy moves along Fisher's [18] vicious spiral. The type of shock that triggers the spiral is irrelevant for the amplification mechanism to be set in motion. A stock market crash or a large loss would reduce the value of banks' assets relative of existing nominal obligations and can trigger the circle. A sunspot can trigger the mechanism as well by selecting the strategies to be played in equilibrium. As soon as banks fail or prices exogenously fall, the amplification mechanism is triggered. Hence, this paper provides a theory of how bank failures are propagated to the real economy rather than a theory of banking panics.

FIGURE 1: Economic Mechanism

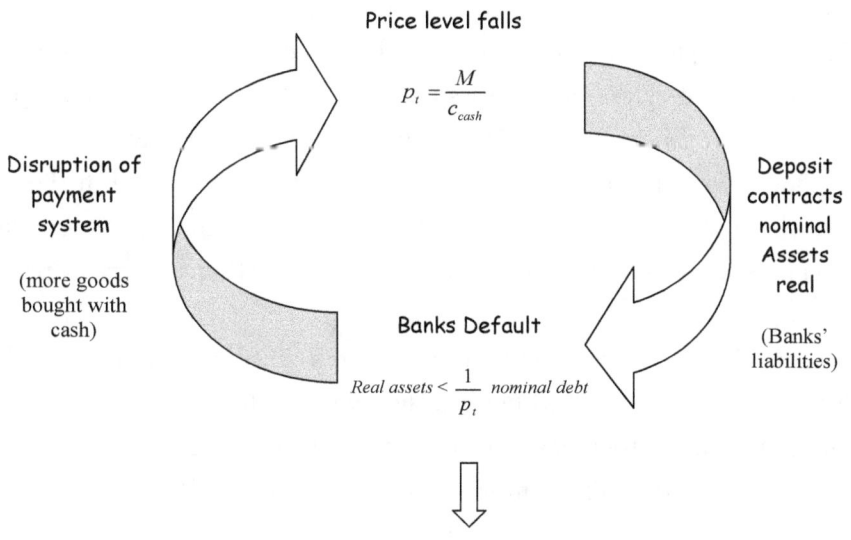

Price level falls

$$p_t = \frac{M}{c_{cash}}$$

Disruption of payment system

(more goods bought with cash)

Deposit contracts nominal Assets real

(Banks' liabilities)

Banks Default

$Real\ assets < \dfrac{1}{p_t}\ nominal\ debt$

New loans fall, Output falls

It is also crucial that deposit contracts not be contingent on the realization of prices at the time the repayment is due for the mismatch in banks' balance sheet to arise. Diamond and Rajan [16] study economies in which repayment on deposits is fixed over the next

5

instant, and compare the effects of a shock to the timing of banks' production in environments with real versus nominal deposit contracts. They show that, under some conditions, nominal deposits may exacerbate real liquidity shortages by increasing aggregate real liquidity demand when supply falls, as in Fisher's [18] debt-deflation argument. So they focus on the right-hand side of the circle in Figure 1.

This paper completes the circle, showing that banking failures and deflation may naturally occur together and are mutually reinforcing. Diamond and Rajan [16] focus on how a specific friction, nominal deposits, amplifies a shock to the timing of banks' production, but in their model there is nothing specific to the operation of the banking system that amplifies liquidity shortages. Their amplification is purely the result of the interaction between nominal deposits with fixed repayment over the next instant and a maturity mismatch in banks' balance sheets.

This paper introduces a role for banks in the amplification mechanism itself: banks provide financial intermediation by issuing liabilities that can be used as means of payment. When such intermediation disappears, aggregate liquidity demand increases, leading prices to fall. Accounting for such feedback effect from bank failures to price dynamics is relevant for two reasons. First, no real shock to banks' balance sheets or output, or the timing of production, is necessary to trigger the amplification, although such a shock would be sufficient to trigger the amplification. Second, consider an economy in which banks play no role in providing payment services but still issue nominal deposits with fixed repayments over the next instant, as in Diamond and Rajan [16]. In such an economy, a drop in output would require a shock of much greater magnitude than would be required in the economy this paper describes, in which once a small shock forces a few banks to fail, the feedback effect on prices causes more banks to fail, and so on with further effects on prices, in a vicious circle.

The paper is organized as follows: section 2 sets up a static version of the full model environment described in section 3, and derives the main result that banking failures and deflation may naturally occur together and are mutually reinforcing. The full dynamic model in section 3 also provides policy implications, after which section 4 concludes.

## 2    One period model

Consider an economy with a continuum of identical households and identical banks, each represented by a Lebesgue measure on the interval $[0, 1]$. Households and banks move

6

simultaneously and they live only for one period. There are three consumption goods: a cash good, a credit good and coconut. Coconut is used as numeraire[14], cash goods can be purchased only using coconut and credit goods can be purchased either with coconut, like cash goods, or with credit. However, regardless of how credit goods are paid for, they are intrinsically different consumption goods from cash goods.

Households' preferences are represented by the utility function $U : \mathbb{R}^3_+ \to \mathbb{R}$ defined over cash good, credit good and coconut: $U(c_1, c_2, A') = \log c_1 + \log c_2 + \log A'$, where $c_1$ denotes the consumption of cash good, $c_2$ the consumption of credit good and $A'$ the consumption of coconut.

Banks' preferences are represented by the utility function $V : \mathbb{R}^2_+ \to \mathbb{R}$ defined over cash and credit goods: $V(c_1^b, c_2^b) = c_1^b + c_2^b$, where $c_1^b$ and $c_2^b$ denote banks' consumption of cash good and credit good respectively[15].

At the beginning of the period banks are endowed with $f$ units of labor. Households are endowed with $y$ units of labor, $A$ units of coconut, and $R$ claims denominated in coconut on each bank that mature at the end of the period[16]. These are claims either payable with coconut or with bank-issue liabilities, as will be explained later.

Households have access to three technologies: they can transform a unit of labor into a unit of either cash or credit good[17], they can carry coconut within the period, and they can plant coconut at the beginning of the period[18], which yields $r > 1$ per unit planted, at the end of the period. Banks can transform a unit of labor into a unit of either cash or credit good. The financial and productive sectors are consolidated in this economy and represented by banks: this is without loss of generality since the crucial assumption is that some agents face a mismatch in the denomination of assets and liabilities, here real assets and nominal liabilities. If banks make nominal loans to firms then firms face such

---

[14]In a static model commodity money relative to fiat money solves the issue of agents not being willing to hold a good without intrinsic value (fiat money) until the end of the period. With preferences defined also over coconut, agents accept coconut for payment and eat it at the end of the period.

[15]It is irrelevant for the results whether banks' preferences are defined over cash good, credit good and coconut like households, or as above. Defining preferences over coconut is useful in a static model because it makes agents willing to accept it for payment. In this setup banks pay households using the coconut they have at the end of the period and offsetting with other banks any households' remaining claims and obligations. If banks' preferences were also defined over coconut then they could eat the coconut and pay households just by offsetting with other banks their claims and obligations, as explained later.

[16]In this static version of the model, households' endowment of $R$ claims on banks play a key role in banks' default decision: they are equivalent to deposits fixed in nominal terms over the next instant in a dynamic model.

[17]As in Lucas-Stokey [23]

[18]In this static version of the model planting coconut is equivalent to depositing money at the bank.

a mismatch: every result in the paper maintains under the assumption that when firms' default on the loans granted by banks, the best a bank can do it to seize the collateral (the real assets of firms). This alternative version of the model is described in a separate online appendix[19].

## 2.1 Households' problem

Similarly to Lucas-Stokey [23] each household is divided into a worker and a shopper: at the beginning of the period the asset market opens and the worker and the shopper make their portfolio decisions together, as a household. Households start the period with an endowment of coconut ($A$) and decide how much of it to carry within the period ($M$) and how much to plant ($D$), which returns $r$ per unit of coconut planted at the end of the period. Banks issue checkbooks, debit and credit cards to households at the beginning of the period against the value of households' income at the end of the period which is directly deposited at the bank. So households can write checks and use debit and credit cards to transfer balances from their account at the bank to other households and banks.

Therefore, at the beginning of the period households face a securities market constraint: $M + D \leq A$. Then the goods' market opens and the worker and the shopper are separated from each other: the shopper takes the coconut that was not planted ($M$) and visits other households and banks to purchase consumption goods. The shopper is constrained to purchase cash goods by paying right away using coconut, whereas she can purchase credit goods by paying right away either with coconut or using checks and cards issued by banks[20].

---

[19]This appendix is available at http://sites.google.com/site/carapellaf/research

[20]In the model credit and debit cards are equivalent as means of payment alternative to cash: they differ only relative to the friction introduced between securities and goods markets. If we assume that there is a timing friction between the instant when income is earned by the worker and the instant when the consumption purchase is made by the shopper, then banks are actually extending credit to households for the time elapsed between the consumption purchase and the receipt of income. So credit goods payments are done by credit cards.

However if we assume that the friction is only physical separation between the shopper and the worker, so that the worker earns income at the same time as the shopper buys consumption goods, but the income is deposited automatically in an account that the household has with a bank, then credit goods payment are done by debit cards, since no credit is extended to the household. In this case, a debit card makes resources that are available in household's portfolios, also available to the physical location where they are needed, that is to say with the shopper.

Because credit and debit cards payments are equivalent in this model, for simplicity they will be referred to as credit payments, as the goods that can be purchased by credit and debit cards are referred to as credit goods.

Her income at the end of the period is given by the return on the coconut planted at the beginning of the period, $(rD)$, the claims on banks $(R)$ and the income from selling goods produced with his endowment of labor $(py$, where $p$ is the price level).

When households pay for credit goods purchases using checks or cards, they have no remaining obligation: banks are responsible to settle those payments[21]. Banks settle payments at the end of the period by netting out their obligations to one another. At this stage (part of) the $R$ claims households have on banks are paid by netting them out with the obligations households have towards banks for paying for credit goods purchases using bank-issued liabilities.

Notice that in this economy when banks are in business and households pay for credit goods using banks-issued liabilities, there is always inside money in the same amount as the value of the credit goods purchased.

On the goods market, households face a cash-in-advance constraint for purchases of cash goods $(pc_1 \leq M)$ and a credit good constraint for purchases of credit goods: $pc_2 \leq M - pc_1 + (1 - \lambda)[py + R + rD]$, where $[py + R + rD]$ denotes household's income at the end of the period, and $\lambda$ the measure of defaulting banks, as defined in (6) and explained later. Credit goods can be purchased with unspent coconut on cash goods, and a fraction, proportional to the measure of non defaulting banks, of household's income at the end of the period. If no banks default $(\lambda = 0)$ then credit goods can be purchased with unspent coconut on cash goods or with credit. If there is a banking crisis and every bank defaults $(\lambda = 1)$ then the credit good constraint implies that credit goods need to be purchased using cash, as well as cash goods, i.e. banks' default implies that the liabilities they issued can no longer be used as means of payment on the goods' market: nobody will accept a check written on a failed bank. The only means of payment available to households to purchase consumption goods is cash.

At the same time as the shopper purchases consumption goods, the worker stays at home and produces cash or credit goods using the labor endowment $y$ and sells them to other households who visit his store.

At the end of the period the shopper returns home and consumption takes place. The coconut consumed at the end of the period $(A')$ is the sum of unspent coconut for the

---

[21]Transactions are authorized at the point of sale, so after authorization is granted the bank is liable to the merchant. For checks it is assumed that households always have enough funds in their accounts to cover the checks they write, which is always the case in equilibrium, or, alternatively, that an electronic authorization procedure is in place at the point of sale for paper checks as well.

purchases of consumption goods $(M - pc_1 - pc_2)$, the return on the coconut planted at the beginning of the period $(rD)$, the claims on $R$ on banks that didn't default and the income from the sale of the endowment $(py)$: $A' \leq M - pc_1 - pc_2 + (1 - \lambda)R + py + rD$.

Therefore households choose $c_1, c_2, A', M, D$ to solve:

$$\max_{\{c_1, c_2, A', M, D\}} U(c_1, c_2, A') \tag{1}$$

$$s.t.$$

$$M + D \leq A \tag{2}$$

$$pc_1 \leq M \tag{3}$$

$$pc_2 \leq M - pc_1 + (1 - \lambda)[R + py + rD] \tag{4}$$

$$A' \leq M - pc_1 - pc_2 + (1 - \lambda)R + py + rD \tag{5}$$

Notice the difference between constraints (4) and (5): suppose that $\lambda = 1$, that is to say every bank defaults. Then constraint (4) implies that when banks' default the financial intermediation that they provide by supplying alternative means of payment to coconut (cash) disappears and the economy turns into a coconut (cash) only economy. However, as shown in (5), households' wealth (coconut) at the end of the period is affected by banks' default only to the extent that households don't receive payment for the $R$ claims they had on banks at the beginning of the period. Households still receive the income from selling their endowment $(py)$ and the return on the coconut they planted $(rD)$ since these are incomes from activities unrelated to banks: $py$ is earned by the worker selling cash and credit goods produced with his labor endowment $y$ at prices $p$, and $rD$ is earned through the planting technology.

## 2.2   Banks' problem

Banks are endowed with an obligation to pay $R$ to households at the end of the period[22], denominated in units of coconut. As pointed out earlier this payment is a combination of units of coconut and credit to households towards the bank, which will are netted out with households obligations towards the bank for using bank-issued liabilities to pay for credit goods. This plays a crucial role in banks' default decision since the value of their existing obligations is fixed to $R$ and cannot be adjusted to reflect changes in the value of banks'

---

[22]Because the equilibrium is later defined as a symmetric equilibrium, it is irrelevant whether banks and households have a one-to-one relationship or each bank deals with arbitrarily many households.

assets. In this static version of the model $R$ is exogenous.

Banks are also endowed with $f$ units of labor, which they can transform into either cash or credit good. When the goods' market opens, banks sell $f$ units of cash or credit goods at price $p$. They are paid either with coconut or with bank-issued liabilities or both[23]. At the end of the period banks settle with one another the liabilities that they issued, and they pay households for their remaining claims[24].

In this static version of the model banks do not make any strategic default decisions, they behave mechanically: if the value of their assets $(pf)$ exceeds the value of their existing nominal obligations $(R)$ then banks are solvent and cannot default, so they pay $R$ to households. Otherwise they do no have enough assets to pay their obligations and default, so households are not paid.

Let $\delta(j)$ be the indicator function that denotes whether bank $j$ defaults ($\delta(j) = 1$ if bank $j$ defaults) and let:

$$\lambda = \int_0^1 \delta(j)dj \tag{6}$$

denote the measure of defaulting banks. Bank $j$'s payoff is then defined by its utility from consuming cash and credit goods, denoted $c_1^b(j), c_2^b(j)$ respectively:

$$V(c_1^b(j), c_2^b(j)) = c_1^b(j) + c_2^b(j) = \begin{cases} f - \frac{R}{p} & \text{if} \quad \delta(j) = 0 \\ f & \text{if} \quad \delta(j) = 1 \end{cases} \tag{7}$$

## 2.3 Equilibrium

**Definition 1** *A symmetric equilibrium is an allocation* $x^* = \{c_1^{b*}, c_2^{b*}, c_1^*, c_2^*, A'^*, M^*, D^*\}$, *a default decision rule for banks* $\delta^*(i) = \delta^*$ $\forall i$, *and prices* $p^*$ *such that:*

*Given prices* $p^*$ *and given a default decision* $\delta^*$ *by banks, the allocation* $x^*$ *solves the*

---

[23] If cash goods are sold then they must be paid with coconut, if credit goods are sold they can be paid either with coconut or banks' issued liabilities. In equilibrium credit goods will be paid with bank-issued liabilities because holding coconut within the period is costly given that households have access to the planting technology at the beginning of the period.

[24] Because bank-issued liabilities are inside money, they are not backed up by coconuts. Therefore from a settlement point of view, when households purchase credit goods from banks and pay with inside money, the value of the credit good purchases they made is deducted from their income at the end of the period, which is directly deposited at the bank. At the same time banks owe households $R$ units of coconut, so they net those obligations of coconuts with the value of credit goods that households purchased, and then pay households for their remaining net claims.

*households' problem (1).*

*Given prices $p^*$ and given the allocation $x^*$ that solves the households' problem (1), banks choose $\delta^*$.*

*Markets clear:*

$$c_1^{b*} + c_2^{b*} + c_1^* + c_2^* = y + f \tag{8}$$

$$A'^* + D^* = rD^* + A \tag{9}$$

where (8) is the goods' market clearing condition: aggregate consumption of cash and credit goods by banks and households equals aggregate production of goods by banks and households, which is just aggregate endowment of labor of banks and households because of the linear production technologies. Equation (9) is the market clearing condition for coconut: aggregate consumption of coconut by households and investment into the planting technology equal the aggregate return on the planting technology and households' initial endowment of coconut.

Under assumptions:

**Assumption 1** $r > 2$

**Assumption 2** $\min(\frac{R(2r-1)}{r(r-3)}, \frac{R(3r-2)y}{2rf}) > A > \frac{R(f+y)(2r-1)}{r(1+r)f}$

**Assumption 3** $y > \frac{f(4r-2)}{3r(r-1)}$

proposition 1 follows:

**Proposition 1** *Let $(r, f, y, R) \in \mathbb{R}_{++}^4$ satisfy assumptions 1 - 3. Then there exist two equilibria: one with banks not defaulting ($\delta^{nd} = 0$), allocation $x^{nd}$ and prices $p^{nd}$; another equilibrium with banks defaulting ($\delta^d = 1$), allocation $x^d$ and prices $p^d$. These equilibria are such that $p^{nd} > p^d$ and households' welfare is higher in no default.*

**Proof** See appendix B.

Proposition 1 shows that bank failures and deflation may naturally occur together in equilibrium and are mutually reinforcing. In the default equilibrium banks fail because prices $p^d$ are so low that even if banks sold all of their assets they still would not be able to pay their existing nominal obligations: $p^d f < R$. When banks fail, constraint (3) is slack and constraint (4) binds so the set of cash goods expands. As a consequence households' need for liquidity (coconut) increases and, absent an increase in the supply of liquidity, there is little cash (coconut) in the economy relative to how many goods households want to purchase with the cash they have. Therefore prices are lower than in the no default equilibrium.

In this static version of the model households' claims on banks ($R$) are exogenous and the return on the coconut planted is independent of banks' survival[25], so that bank failures do not affect households' willingness to plant some of their endowment of coconut ($D^d > 0$). This has two implications. First, it is costly for households to hold cash regardless of whether banks default or not, so that the relevant cash in advance constraint always binds[26]. Second, a lower bound on $R$ is necessary for households' welfare to be higher in the no default equilibrium. This is because in the default equilibrium households suffer a utility loss from the effects of financial disintermediation on allocations and prices and from the loss of wealth ($R$ claims on banks). However there is a utility gain caused by equalizing the marginal rate of substitution between cash and credit goods with the marginal rate of transformation because the relevant cash-in-advance constraint binds on both goods. Therefore, households enjoy higher utility in the no default equilibrium if and only if the utility loss in default is large enough, as required by assumption 2.

## 3   Dynamic Model

This section provides a framework in which banking is built in a standard macroeconomic model. The framework fleshes out the features of the environment which capture the main aspects of the banking crisis that occurred in the United States before the establishment of federal deposit insurance: prices declined, output fell and a wave of bank failures precipitated. Such a framework is also suitable to be employed in several applications: introducing heterogeneity among banks would generate contagion[27] and it would permit quantitative evaluations of specific policies.

For analytical tractability this paper focuses on a stationary equilibrium in which banks

---

[25] In the dynamic model households deposit their money at the bank rather than planting coconuts, so that the return on deposits depend on banks being in business: when banks fail, households are not paid and stop depositing, so a banking panic occurs.

[26] In the dynamic version of model, as long as households' preference discount factor is smaller than 1 ($\beta < 1$) then the implicit intertemporal interest rate is larger than the return to holding money, as in Lucas and Stokey [23]: cash is costly to hold and households' optimization implies that they will minimize cash holdings.

[27] After a few banks fail, prices start to fall thus inducing more banks to fail.

operate profitably until a shock hits, triggering a banking crisis that results in banks failing and disappearing. So there is no banking system after the shock hits.

The model economy is a dynamic game with a continuum of identical households and identical banks, each represented by a Lebesgue measure on the interval $[0, 1]$. Households are anonymous players in the game, whereas banks are not: the history of their past actions is publicly observable. There are two consumption goods, a cash good ($c_1$) and a credit good ($c_2$), and fiat money. Time is discrete and infinite.

## 3.1  Households

Similarly to Lucas-Stokey [23], households' preferences are defined over cash and credit goods and are represented by the utility function $U : R_+^2 \to R_+$, with $U_i > 0, i = 1, 2$ and $U_{ii} < 0, i = 1, 2$. At the beginning of every period households are endowed with $y$ units of labor and $A$ units of money. They have access to a technology that allows them to transform one unit of labor endowment into one unit of either cash or credit good. Households can transfer wealth intertemporally either by holding money or by depositing money at banks[28]. The timing and constraints related to securities and goods' market are exactly the same as in the one-period model. Also, households' income is directly deposited into their accounts at each bank, as in the one-period model.

## 3.2  Banks

The financial and productive sectors in this economy are consolidated and represented by banks. Bankers are entrepreneurs at the same time: they have access to a productive technology and operate it. Banks' preferences are defined as in the one-period model. Let $\gamma$ denote banks' discount factor.

Banks have a fixed endowment of labor $L$ in every period, and they have access to a productive technology $f : R_+^2 \to R_+$, $f$ is strictly increasing and $f_i(0, \cdot) = f_i(\cdot, 0) = 0, i = 1, 2$, whose inputs are an investment of cash good[29] and the fixed factor $L$.

Banks offer deposit contracts to households and carry out production competitively. Deposit contracts cannot be contingent on the realization of prices at the time when re-

---

[28]Results are independent on whether households and banks sign a one-to-one deposit contract or households hold a diversified portfolio of deposits at every bank because the focus is on symmetric equilibria.

[29]This assumption is not crucial: none of the results would change if the input to the productive technology were a credit good.

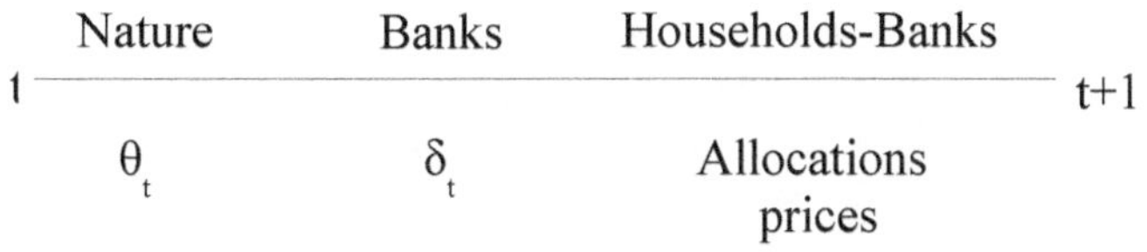

FIGURE 2: Timing of players' moves

payments by banks are due: the interest rate on deposits is thus fixed in nominal terms, although it is endogenous.

As in the one-period model, banks issue checks, debit and credit cards to households up to the face value of household's income at the end of each period, which is the gross return on deposits and the income from selling cash and credit goods produced with the labor endowment $y$.

## 3.3 Timing of players' moves

At the beginning of every period the outcome of a sunspot, denoted $\theta_t$, is publicly observed (see Figure 2). $\theta_t$ has range $\{0, 1\}$ and distribution $\Pi$: $\Pi(\theta_t = 0) = \pi$, $\Pi(\theta_t = 1) = (1 - \pi)$. The sunspot hits at time $t$ if $\theta_t = 1$.

At time $t$, after the realization of the sunspot, $\theta_t$, banks simultaneously choose whether to default: if they do not default, they sell the output from the productive technology on the goods market and pay households the promised interest rate on deposits. If banks default depositors are not paid[30]. Similarly to the one period model, the default decision of bank $j$ at time $t$ is denoted $\delta_t(j)$.

After banks have decided whether to default, they decide how many deposits to offer $(D_t^b)$ and how much to invest in the productive technology and households choose consumption allocation $(c_{1t}, c_{2t})$ and asset holdings $(M_t, D_t)$. At the end of the period, if banks do not default, then depositors are paid the promised interest rate on the deposits made in the previous period $(R_{t-1}D_{t-1})$.

The stage game is represented in extensive form in Figure 3, where, after Nature has

---

[30]Allowing banks to keep their assets when they default on their liabilities is not crucial: it is however crucial that when banks default the payment system gets disrupted and households must use cash to pay for their consumption purchases. If banks' assets were seized and rebated to households after a liquidation process of the banks takes place, the key results of the paper would not be affected as long as during the liquidation process households cannot use the checks and the debit and credit cards that banks had issued to them.

15

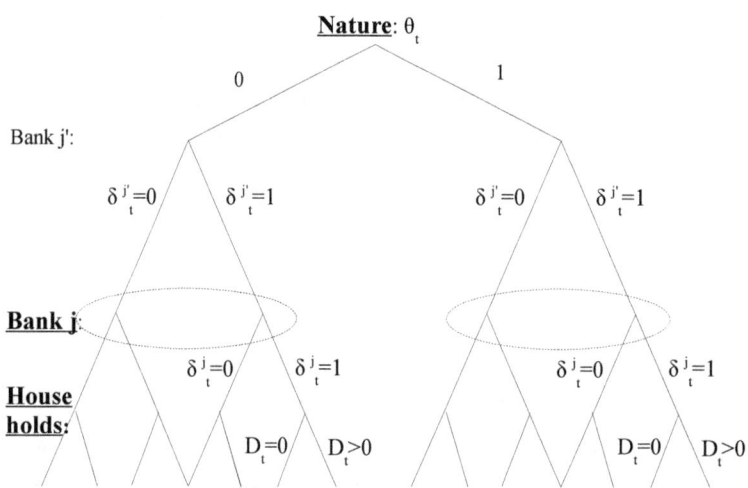

FIGURE 3: Stage Game in extensive form

drawn a realization of $\theta_t$, bank $j$ chooses whether to default without knowing what other banks $j'$ chose: then households choose consumption allocation and asset holdings and banks choose how much to invest in the productive technology. In particular households choose whether to deposit a strictly positive amount of assets. For analytical tractability it is assumed that when a bank defaults then it loses its endowment of labor $L$ forever. Hence when $\lambda_t = \int_0^1 \delta_t(j)dj = 1$, then the banking system shuts down forever: the only source of output in the economy is households' endowment and the only means of payment available to households is cash.

## 3.4  Players' strategies

Let $h^{t-1}$ denote the history of the game at the beginning of time $t$. $h^{t-1}$ is anonymous with respect to households, which are anonymous players in the game, and is a list of past default decisions by every bank $j \in [0,1]$ $(\delta_s(j)_{j\in[0,1]})$, sunspot realizations $(\theta_t)$, prices of consumption goods $(p_s)$ and deposits $(R_s)$, aggregate asset holdings by households at the beginning of every period $(A_s)$, aggregate consumption of cash good $(c_{1s})$, of credit good $(c_{2s})$, aggregate cash $(M_s)$ and deposits holdings at every bank $j$ $(D_s(j))$:
$$h^{t-1} = (\delta_s(j)_{j\in[0,1]}, \theta_s, p_s, R_s, A_s, c_{1s}, c_{2s}, i_s, M_s, D_s(j)_{j\in[0,1]} \mid s \leq t-1).$$

Let $h_1^t = (h^{t-1}, \theta_t, \delta_t(j)_{j\in[0,1]})$ denote the history of the game at time $t$ after banks' default decisions have been made, which includes the history at the beginning of period $t$, the current realization of the sunspot $(\theta_t)$ and the current default decision of every bank $j$ $(\delta_t(j)_{j\in[0,1]})$.

Let the set of possible histories at the beginning of time $t$ be denoted $H^t$, with $H^0 = \emptyset$, and the set of possible histories at time $t$ after banks' default decisions have been made be denoted $H_1^t$ with $H_1^0 = \{\theta_0, \delta_0(j)_{j\in[0,1]}\}$, so that $h_1^t$ is a typical element of $H_1^t$.

A strategy for a household is a mapping $\sigma_t^H : H_1^t \to \mathbb{R}_+^5$. After history $h_1^t$ is realized, households' strategy is $\sigma_t^H(h_1^t) = \{(c_{1t}(h_1^t), c_{2t}(h_1^t), D_t(h_1^t), M_t(h_1^t), A_{t+1}(h_1^t)) \in \mathbb{R}_+^5\}$ and a strategy profile for a representative household is denoted: $\sigma^H = \{\sigma_t^H\}_{t=0}^\infty$.

Let $\mu_t^H : H_1^{t+1} \to [0,1]$ denote the conditional probability [31] that history $h_1^{t+1} \succ h_1^t$ will be realized if $h_1^t$ is the realized history at time $t$. Then a household that starts period $t$ with assets $A_t$ and deposits $D_{t-1}$, chooses $\{c_{1t}, c_{2t}, M_t, D_t, A_{t+1}\}$ to maximize her payoff at time $t$ after history $h_1^t$ has been observed, denoted $v_t(h_1^t, A_t, D_{t-1})$:

$$v_t(h_1^t, A_t, D_{t-1}) = \max\left\{U(c_{1t}, c_{2t}) + \beta \int_{h^{t+1}\in H^{t+1}} \mu_t(h_1^{t+1} \mid h_1^t) v_{t+1}(h_1^{t+1}, A_{t+1}, D_t) dh^{t+1}\right\} \quad (10)$$
$$s.t.$$

$$M_t + D_t = A_t \quad (11)$$

$$p_t(H^t)c_{1t} \leq M_t \quad (12)$$

$$p_t(H^t)\left(c_{1t} + c_{2t}\right) \leq M_t + (1-\lambda_t)\left(p_t(H^t)y_t + R_{t-1}(H^{t-1})D_{t-1}\right) \quad (13)$$

$$A_{t+1} = M_t - p_t(H^t)c_{1t} - p_t(H^t)c_{2t}$$
$$+ p_t(H^t)y_t + (1-\lambda_t)R_{t-1}(H^{t-1})D_{t-1} \quad (14)$$

As in the one-period-model, constraint (11) is the securities market constraint: the household splits his assets between cash to carry within the period and deposits at banks. Constraint (12) is the cash-in-advance constraint on cash goods and constraint (13) is the credit good constraint. Credit goods can be purchased with unspent cash on cash goods, and with a fraction, proportional to the measure of non defaulting banks, of the income from the sales of the endowment and the return on previous period deposits, which are paid to the households at the end of the period[32]. Because both are paid at the end of the

---

[31] induced by the sunspot distribution and players' strategies.

[32] As noted in section 2.1 every result is independent of the type of friction introduced between the securities and the goods' market. Both a timing friction and physical separation between the worker and the shopper imply that households' income is not available on the goods' market and that financial intermediation provided by banks allows households to carry into the period only the cash they need to purchase cash goods.

period, they could not be used to pay for consumption purchases if banks were not providing intermediation by issuing liabilities that can be used as means of payment. Finally, constraint (14) is the law of motion for assets: assets at the beginning of the next period are unspent cash, income from the sales of the endowment and a fraction, proportional to the measure of non defaulting banks, of the return on previous period deposits. As in the one-period-model, when banks default households lose the return on deposits made in the previous period but don't lose their income as a form of wealth: households will still get paid for the sales of their endowment at the end of the period, because that income stems from an activity unrelated to banks.

At the first information set where they move, banks choose whether to default or not; at the second information set where they move, banks choose investment into the productive technology $(i_t(j)(h_1^t))$ and deposits $(D_t^b(j)(h_1^t))$ to offer households. A strategy for banks is a mapping $\sigma_t^B(h_1^t) : H^{t-1} \times H_1^t \to \{0,1\} \times \mathbb{R}_+^2$, so after history $h_1^t = (h^{t-1}, \theta_t, \delta_t(j)_{j\in[0,1]})$ is realized, bank $j$ strategy is $\sigma_t^B(j)(h_1^t) = \{\delta_t(j)(h^{t-1}, \theta_t), i_t(j)(h_1^t), D_t^b(j)(h_1^t)\}$ and a strategy profile is $\sigma^B = \{\sigma_t^B(j)_{j\in[0,1]}\}_{t=0}^\infty$.

If the real value of banks' liabilities exceeds the real value of their assets $(f(i_{t-1}, L) < \frac{R_{t-1}D_{t-1}^b}{p_t})$ then banks must default because even if they sold all of their assets at time $t$ they still could not pay their time $t$ obligations. This is an involuntary default. If the real value of banks' assets is sufficient to cover the real value of their liabilities $(f(i_{t-1}, L) \geq \frac{R_{t-1}D_{t-1}^b}{p_t})$ then the bank chooses whether to default or not. Let $W_t^j(h^{t-1}, \theta_t, \delta_t(j))$ denote the payoff to bank $j$ at time $t$ choosing $\delta_t(j)$ after observing history $h^{t-1}$ and sunspot realization $\theta_t$. Then:

$$W_t^j(h^{t-1}, \theta_t, \delta_t(j)) = \begin{cases} f(i_{t-1}, L) - \frac{R_{t-1}D_{t-1}^b}{p_t} + \gamma w_{t+1}^j(h_1^t) & \text{if } \delta_t(j) = 0 \\ f(i_{t-1}, L) & \text{if } \delta_t(j) = 1 \end{cases}$$

where $\gamma$ is banks' discount factor and $w_{t+1}^j(h_1^t)$ the value of bank $j$ expected profits at time $t+1$ after history $h_1^t$. Therefore, bank $j$ chooses to default $(\delta_t(j) = 1)$ if $\frac{R_{t-1}D_{t-1}^b}{p_t} > \gamma w_{t+1}^j(h_1^t)$ and no to default otherwise.

If they did not default, then banks choose how many deposits to sell and how much to invest in the productive technology to maximize expected profits:

$$w_{t+1}^j(h_1^t) = \max_{\{i_t, D_t^b\}} E_{\theta_{t+1}|\theta_t}[W_{t+1}^j(h^t, \theta_{t+1}, \delta_{t+1}(j)) \mid \sigma^B, \sigma^H] \tag{15}$$

$$s.t. \qquad p_t i_t \leq D_t^b \tag{16}$$

18

Constraint (16) is banks' budget constraint: investment into productive projects is financed by the deposits they sold to households[33]

## 3.5 Equilibrium characterization

**Definition 2** *A subgame perfect symmetric equilibrium is:*

1. *a symmetric strategy profile for households $\sigma^H = \{\sigma_t^H\}_{t=0}^\infty$*

2. *a symmetric strategy profile for banks $\sigma^B = \{\sigma_t^B\}_{t=0}^\infty$*

3. *pricing functions $p_t(h_1^t), R_t(h_1^t)$[34]*

*such that for any $t, h_1^t$, households maximize; for any $t, h^t$, banks maximize and prices clear the markets:*

$$c_t^b(h_1^t) + c_{1t}(h_1^t) + c_{2t}(h_1^t) + i_t(h_1^t) = y_t + f(i_{t-1}(h_1^{t-1}), L) \tag{17}$$

$$M_t(h_1^t) + D_t(h_1^t) = \overline{M}_t = \overline{M} \tag{18}$$

The resource constraint (17) indicates that aggregate consumption by banks and households, and aggregate investment in the productive technology equal output of cash and credit good produced by households with labor endowment $y_t$, and the output from banks' productive technology using $t-1$ inputs. The money market clearing condition (18) indicates that aggregate cash and deposit holdings by households equal the stock of money supply at time $t$.

Consider equilibria with constant money supply ($\overline{M}_t = \overline{M}$) and let $U(c_1, c_2) = \log(c_1) + \log(c_2)$ and $f(i_t, L) = i_t^\alpha L^{1-\alpha}$. Further assume:

**Assumption 4** $[\alpha\beta^2 L^{1-\alpha}\pi]^{\frac{1}{1-\alpha}} < y$

**Assumption 5** $1 + [2\beta(1-\pi) + \beta\pi \frac{[(\frac{y\alpha}{\pi})^{1-\alpha} + 2(1-\pi)\alpha\beta^2 L^{1-\alpha}]}{[(\frac{y\alpha}{\pi})^{1-\alpha} - \pi\alpha\beta^2 L^{1-\alpha}]}]^{-1} > \frac{\pi}{\alpha} + (\frac{L}{y})^{1-\alpha}\frac{[\alpha\beta^2 L^{1-\alpha}(2-\pi)]^\alpha}{[y^{1-\alpha} + 2(1-\pi)\alpha\beta^2 L^{1-\alpha}]^\alpha}$

---

[33]A large business cycle literature focuses on the role of credit market frictions on output fluctuations. Such frictions affect firms' borrowing constraint when undertaking investment projects: see Bernanke and Gertler [4], Bernanke, Gertler and Gilchrist [5], and Carlstrom and Fuerst [10]. This is formalized in the model by assuming that banks' discount factor $\gamma$ is small enough so that bankers consume their profits in every period, as guaranteed by assumption 7. See also appendix C.

[34]Notice that pricing functions are defined over aggregate histories: $\mathbb{H}^t = (h^{t-1}, \theta_t, \int_0^1 \delta_t(j)dj)$. However aggregate histories are functions of $h_1^t = (h^{t-1}, \theta_t, (\delta_t(j))_{j\in[0,1]})$, since they are defined over the aggregate default decisions by banks rather than on each bank $j$ default decision. Therefore ultimately pricing functions $p_t$ and $R_t$ are functions of $h_1^t$.

**Assumption 6** $\frac{\alpha}{\pi} < 1$

**Assumption 7** *Either* $\gamma < \beta^2$ *or* $\gamma > \beta^2(2 - \pi)$

**Assumption 8** $\frac{\alpha(1-\gamma\pi)}{\pi\gamma(1-\alpha)} < 1$

Under the above assumptions there exists a symmetric equilibrium in this economy such that no default occurs until the first date $t$ at which the sunspot hits ($\theta_t = 1$): then banks fail, households don't deposit in any bank, prices decline and aggregate output falls. There is no banking system after that[35].

**Proposition 2** *Let $t$ denote the first date at which the sunspot hits ($\theta_t = 1$). If Assumptions 4-6 are satisfied then there exists a symmetric equilibrium such that:*

- $\lambda_s = \int_0^1 \delta_s(j)dj = 0$, $D_s(j) = D^{nd} > 0$ $\forall j \in [0,1]$, $p_s = p^{nd}$, $\quad \forall s < t$

- $\lambda_s = \int_0^1 \delta_s(j)dj = 1$, $D_s(j) = 0$ $\forall j \in [0,1]$, $p_s = p^d$, $\quad \forall s \geq t$

- $p^d < p^{nd}$

- $Y_s = \begin{cases} y & \forall s \geq t+1 \\ y + f(i(h_1^s), L) & \forall s \leq t \end{cases}$

**Proof** See Appendix B.

Proposition 2 generalizes proposition 1 to a dynamic environment where banks make strategic default decisions, and where deposits and banks' production are explicitly linked. Banks default when the actual price is too low relative to the price their nominal liabilities are indexed to, and when banks default the payment services they would normally provide are no longer viable. The only means of payment available in the economy is now cash, causing the set of goods that are purchased using cash to expand. To the extent that the ratio of goods purchased by cash to the amount of cash brought within the period is larger than in no default, then prices fall.

Also, because the deposit decision is dynamic and influenced by the probability that the bank will not be insolvent, this version of the model highlights the impact of a banking

---

[35]This is done for analytical tractability. Letting banks come back in business after failing or letting new banks enter the market after banking failures have occurred, would require evaluating banks' continuation payoffs at allocations that are not time invariant.

panic on investment and ultimately on aggregate output. When banks fail, households are not paid and do not deposit their assets at any bank, so a banking panic occurs[36]. No investment into the productive technology $f$ takes place, since deposits are the only source of funds for banks to purchase production inputs, so aggregate output falls.

## 3.6 Monetary policy and the Friedman and Schwartz hypothesis

This section analyzes the relationship between banking and monetary policy.

In the environment described in sections 3.1-3.5 consider a monetary authority endowed with a printing money technology, who can commit to future policies and moves after banks decided whether to default or not, so the relevant history of the game at its information set is $h_1^t$.

For analytical tractability the focus is on a one time policy experiment in period $\widehat{t}$. Let the economy start from the equilibrium described in proposition 2 so that banks' existing deposits $D_{\widehat{t}-1} = D^{nd}$. Let the monetary authority adopt the following active policy: if a positive measure of banks defaults at time $\widehat{t}$ then it injects cash on the securities market to households in the amount $T_{\widehat{t}}(h_1^{\widehat{t}})$, otherwise it leaves $\overline{M}$ unchanged. The amount of the money injection $T_{\widehat{t}}(h_1^{\widehat{t}})$ is just enough to keep current prices constant with respect to the previous period, and is a function of the measure of banks that defaulted at the beginning of the period. If a measure one of banks defaults ($\lambda_{\widehat{t}} = 1$) then $T_{\widehat{t}}(h_1^{\widehat{t}}) = p^{nd}y - \overline{M}$ so that the new stock of money supply is $\overline{M}'(h_1^{\widehat{t}}) = \overline{M} + T_{\widehat{t}}(h_1^{\widehat{t}}) = p^{nd}y$. Then time $\widehat{t}$ prices in equilibrium are $p_{\widehat{t}} = p^{nd}$ because when the banking system collapses ($\lambda_{\widehat{t}} = 1$) any consumption good that households buy must be paid in cash (their cash in advance constraint is $p_{\widehat{t}}(c_{1\widehat{t}} + c_{2\widehat{t}}) = \overline{M}'(h_1^{\widehat{t}})$), and they buy a total of $y$ goods. If a smaller measure of banks defaults then the cash transfer necessary to keep prices at no-default level ($p^{nd}$) will be smaller. Proposition 3 shows that if the monetary authority follows this active policy, then when the sunspot hits it is no longer optimal for banks to default.

**Proposition 3** *Under assumptions 4-6 the unique pure strategy equilibrium with an active monetary policy is no default and no panics at time $0$ and no decline in economic activity.*

**Proof** See appendix B.

---

[36]Because the focus is not what drives depositors to run on banks, banking panics in this model are identified with households not being paid for the claims they had on banks.

This result shows that the Friedman-Schwartz hypothesis is correct in this environment: an active monetary policy would have been effective in the early 1930s at preventing prices from falling and banking panics from occurring. By avoiding massive bank failures, an active monetary policy would have prevented the collapse of the stock of money and the banking system, thus resulting in a milder cycle[37].

Monetary policy in this environment is very powerful: banking crises arise solely from a fall in prices because banks' liabilities are fixed in nominal terms. Because prices are determined in the market for cash goods, by affecting the stock of money that is brought to the goods' market, the monetary authority can influence prices. The commitment by the monetary authority to keep prices constant is enough to give banks incentives not to default, therefore no failures and no deflation occur in equilibrium. Depositors do not panic and economic activity does not decline. Commitment to price stability is sufficient to discipline off equilibrium payoffs and sustain no default in equilibrium, with no actual money injections taking place.

## 3.7 Deposit Insurance

This section studies the effectiveness of deposit insurance in the environment described in sections 3.1-3.5 and evaluates it relative to the monetary policy described in section 3.6. If coupled with strict regulatory arrangements deposit insurance can prevent banking panics. Absent strict regulatory arrangements, deposit insurance can prevent banking panics but also induces larger output fluctuations than monetary policy interventions, because it induces moral hazard on the part of banks.

In order to study moral hazard incentives for banks, let the set of productive technologies that banks can invest in include both the safe technology introduce in section 3.5, $f(i_t, L) = i_t^\alpha L^{1-\alpha}$, and a risky technology: $\widehat{f}(i_t, L) = \widehat{r} i_t^\alpha L^{1-\alpha}$ where $\widehat{r}$ is a random variable defined over a probability space $(\Omega, \mathcal{F}, P)$, so that $\widehat{r} : \Omega \to X = \{\underline{r}, \overline{r}\}$ with $\overline{r} > 1$[38]. Define $\overline{A} = \{\omega \in \Omega : \widehat{r}(\omega) = \overline{r}\}$ as the event where the risky technology has high return, $\overline{r}$. The distribution of $\widehat{r}$ is $P(\overline{A}) = q$ and $P(\overline{A}^C) = 1 - q$. $\widehat{r}$ is an aggregate shock and it is such that $q\overline{r} + (1-q)\underline{r} < 1$ so that $\widehat{f}$ is a mean reducing spread of $f$. Also, $\widehat{r}$ is independent of the sunspot and $i.i.d$ over time.

For analytical tractability the focus is on a one-time policy experiment in period $\widehat{t}$.

---

[37]See Friedman and Schwartz [19], in *The Great Contraction- Origin of Bank Failures*.

[38]If $\overline{r} \leq 1$ then there are no interesting trade offs since banks would always choose $f$ because it dominates $\widehat{f}$ in every state of the world.

FIGURE 4: Timing of the game with deposit insurance

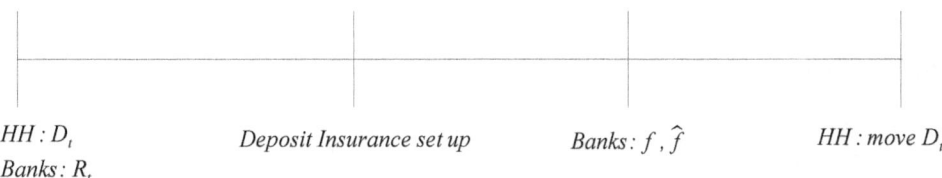

HH : $D_t$          *Deposit Insurance set up*         *Banks:* $f, \hat{f}$        HH : move $D_t$

Banks: $R_t$

Let the economy start at time 0 with initial deposits $D^{nd}$ as defined in proposition 2. Define a deposit insurance mechanism as a set of rules that govern transfers between a deposit insurer, banks and depositors: the deposit insurer seizes banks' assets if they default and pays depositors the amount they were promised every time banks fail. If there are resources left over after paying depositors back, then those resources are rebated back to banks in lump sum, whereas if resources are not sufficient to pay depositors, the deposit insurer levies a lump sum tax on households' endowment to finance the remaining payments. Deposit insurance is set up after households' deposit decision but before banks' choice of technology. After observing the choice of technology by banks, households can move their deposits to a different bank[39]. So the timing of players' actions is represented in figure 4.

When banks' liabilities are taken over by the deposit insurer, the payment instruments that failing banks issued to households are still viable, to the extent that failing banks have enough real resources to cover the real value of their liabilities at the price level anticipated when the liability originated. This happens if and only if $f \geq \frac{R_{t-1}D_{t-1}}{\hat{p}_t}$, where $\hat{p}_t$ is the time $t$ price level as anticipated in the deposit contract signed at $t - 1$[40].

Modify assumptions 5 and 6 from the section 3.5 as follows:

---

[39]This choice of timing is equivalent to having competitive banks choose the productive technology at the very beginning of the period, households observing that decision and then deciding whether to deposit in that bank or not. However, renegotiation of the deposit contract, taking advantage of a potential situation of market power by a deviating bank, is ruled out in order to keep the analysis analytically tractable.

[40]If banks' assets, however, are not sufficient to cover their liabilities at the price level that was anticipated when the deposit contract was signed, then deposit insurance cannot guarantee that payment instruments issued by banks' are still viable, because that would no longer be equivalent to guaranteeing banks' liabilities, but it would imply guaranteeing that households will extend a line of credit to each other in the same amount as the payment instruments that banks had issued.

Notice that assuming means of payment are still viable when deposit insurance takes on banks' liabilities is necessary to obtain that deposit insurance prevents bank failures to cause deflation and consequently trigger the amplification mechanism, even in an environment with strict regulations where the real value of banks' assets does not fall (i.e. output from $f$ does not fall).

**Assumption 9** $1+[2\beta(1-\pi)+\beta\pi\frac{[(\frac{y\alpha}{\pi\bar{r}})^{1-\alpha}+2(1-\pi)\alpha\beta^2L^{1-\alpha}]}{[(\frac{y\alpha}{\pi\bar{r}})^{1-\alpha}-\pi\alpha\beta^2L^{1-\alpha}]}]^{-1} > \frac{\pi\bar{r}}{\alpha}+\bar{r}(\frac{L}{y})^{1-\alpha}\frac{[\alpha\beta^2L^{1-\alpha}(2-\pi)]^{\alpha}}{[y^{1-\alpha}+2(1-\pi)\alpha\beta^2L^{1-\alpha}]^{\alpha}}$

**Assumption 10** $\frac{\alpha E(\hat{r})}{q\pi} < 1$

Let $z = \frac{\gamma(1-\alpha)}{1-\gamma\pi} - \frac{\alpha}{\pi}$ and further assume:

**Assumption 11** $q > \underline{q} = \frac{1+z}{\bar{r}+z}$

The following proposition draws results on the effectiveness of deposit insurance at preventing banking panics, and on its effects on output and prices. Deposit insurance is analyzed in two regulatory environments: one with strict regulations, where the insurer can force banks to invest only in the safe technology, and one without strict regulations, where banks cannot be forced to invest in a specific technology.

**Proposition 4** *If assumptions 4,7-11 are satisfied then:*

1. *Without deposit insurance the unique pure strategy equilibrium is for banks to invest in the safe technology $f$,*

2. *with deposit insurance and with strict regulations then no default and no panics at time 0 is the unique pure strategy equilibrium*

3. *with deposit insurance but without strict regulations then the unique pure strategy equilibrium at time 0 is such that:*

   - *banks invest in the risky technology $\hat{f}$,*
   - *banks do not default and households do not panic if $\hat{r} = \bar{r}$,*
   - *banks default but households are paid if $\hat{r} = \underline{r}$.*

**Proof** See appendix B.

Because the deposit insurer takes on banks' liabilities in a bad state of the world, without affecting bank's profits in a good state of the world, it creates moral hazard. Banks have incentives to invest in riskier assets if the deposit insurer cannot force banks to invest in the safe technology: in good states of the world aggregate output is high and in bad states of the world it is low. Therefore deposit insurance amplifies business cycle

24

fluctuations. If the deposit insurer could force banks to invest only in the safe technology, then it would achieve the same outcome as a monetary policy aimed at keeping prices constant (proposition 4.2). Also, proposition 4.1 guarantees that none of the results in propositions 2 and 3 change when banks are allowed to choose between $f$ and $\hat{f}$: without deposit insurance banks choose to invest in the safe technology $f$: propositions 2 and 3 go through.

The results in proposition 4 contribute to the literature that studies the tradeoffs associated with deposit insurance. Previous work has mostly focused on designing appropriate incentive schemes to control the moral hazard induced by insurance; some research has pointed out alternative policies to deposit insurance that do not induce moral hazard, under certain conditions.

This paper takes a different approach: it points out an additional channel through which moral hazard can be very costly. Deposit insurance may trigger the amplification mechanism of banking failures through deflation to the extent that it does not *always*[41] guarantee that payments by checks and cards issued by failed banks will be honored. If such payments cannot be honored, then even in an environment with strict regulations deposit insurance cannot achieve the same equilibrium outcome as the monetary policy of proposition 3, because any sunspot realization may trigger the vicious circle. In an environment without strict regulations, any low realization of banks' risky technology triggers the circle, because in this state of the world deposit insurance cannot guarantee that payment instruments issued by failing banks are still viable.

# 4 Conclusion

Starting with Fisher's [18] debt-deflation theory of the Great Depression and subsequently Friedman and Schwartz's [19] seminal work on the monetary history of the United States, monetary forces were considered a potent instrument for promoting economic stability, by preventing or moderating large price declines.

Later work has focused on the role of banks in the provision of liquidity and their fragility due to the maturity transformation banks provide: this literature has helped

---

[41]Suppose for instance that the resources deposit insurance can gather by taxing households are not sufficient to cover payments to depositors: then banks' liabilities cannot be guaranteed, and so checks and cards payments. One such example is when households' production is a random variable correlated with $\hat{r}$, such that if at time $t$ $\hat{r}_t = \underline{r}$ then $y_t$ is low, so low that the insurer cannot feasibly raise enough resources to pay depositors.

understanding the economic rationale for many institutional arrangements that took place after the Great Depression and even challenged them ([15], [11], [13], [17], [21], [24]).

Recent work placed banks' fragility along another perspective drawing from Fisher's [18] idea: the existence of frictions in contracting prevents state contingent repayment on deposits. Any shock that was not anticipated at the time the deposit contract was signed may impair banks' solvency. Therefore monetary intervention can help offset monetary and real shocks by keeping the price level stable, thus limiting the future real repayment obligations of banks ([16]).

This paper further investigates such a mechanism showing that when repayment on deposit contracts is fixed in nominal terms over the next instant, and when banks provide financial intermediation through payment services, banking difficulties may be endogenously amplified, in a vicious circle. When banks' payment services decrease, households' demand for cash increases, which induces prices to fall. When prices fall, the real burden of existing nominal obligations increases relative to assets, leading banks to be illiquid and fail.

In this environment monetary intervention is very powerful: adjusting the supply of liquidity to aggregate conditions, it prevents the amplification mechanism from being triggered, ensuring that the banking system is not destabilized. Because price declines are the cause of bank failures, deposit insurance cannot tackle the root of the problem, to the extent that it doesn't affect prices to counteract changes in aggregate liquidity conditions. Nonetheless, by insuring banks' liabilities it still prevents panics, in the sense that depositors are paid their claims on banks. By insuring banks' liabilities, however, deposit insurance induces moral hazard, thus resulting in larger business cycle fluctuation than monetary policy would.

This suggests an important role for monetary policy in stabilizing the banking system. It also suggests that further investigation of the frictions that lead to difficulties in contracting resulting in fixed repayments should be fostered, as well as mechanisms that, given those frictions, may be welfare improving relative to fixed repayment arrangements[42].

---

[42]The trade off between real versus nominal contracts is analyzed by Diamond and Rajan [16] but they still assume contracts with a fixed repayment over the next instant.

# A Appendix

## A.1 United States between 1837 and 1933

Table A.1 reports stylized evidence that every major banking panic in the US in the time frame $1837 - 1933$ was associated with a downturn in economic activity, and that typically the banking panics that were associated with larger price declines were also associated with more significant declines in economic activity. In Table A.1 price declines are measured by the percentage change in the wholesale prices index (Warren and Pearson, [31]) and slowdown in economic activity is measured by the percentage change in pig iron production as a proxy for industrial production (Gorton, [20]). Also, evidence from Sprague [26] shows

TABLE A.1: Banking Panics, Deflations and Recessions in the US: 1837-1933

| Panic date | $\Delta$ Wholesale Prices(%)[a] | $\Delta$Pig Iron (%)[b] |
|---|---|---|
| May 1837 | −13 (1836-1838) | na |
| May 1857 | −13 (1857-1858) | na |
| Sept. 1873 | −30 (1873-1879) | −51 |
| Jun. 1884 | −20 (1882-1885) | −14 |
| May 1893 | −15 (1892-1894) | −29 |
| Oct. 1896 | −7 (1895-1897) | −4 |
| Oct. 1907 | −6 (1907-1908) | −46.5 |
| 1929-33 | −30[c] | −50[c] |

[a]Warren and Pearson [31] , [b]Gorton [20] , [c] Friedman and Schwartz [19]

that the banking panics of 1873, 1884 and 1907 in the United States were all accompanied by a fall in the price level: typically the decline in prices of agricultural goods was more relevant than others, because of the extent to which it affected the value of banks' assets. Friedman and Schwartz [19] report that between 1865 and 1879 wholesale prices fell continuously at a rate approaching 6.5% a year, with a sharper decline of over 30% between 1873 and 1879 (p.30,32,42) when a banking panic occurred; between 1882 and 1885 they fell over 20%, with the panic starting in 1884 (p.94); between 1892 and 1894 they fell roughly 15%, with bank runs precipitating in 1893 (p.94,108); the banking panic of October 1907 was associated with a fall in prices that reached a monthly rate of 5% (p.156).

The decline in real activity was also substantial: during the panic of 1873, loans by national banks fell on average 9% and during the panic of 1907 they fell on average 2%

(Sprague, 1910, p.305-310).

For the banking panics that occurred during the Great Depression Friedman and Schwartz [19] offer a detailed description of the extent of the fall in prices and economic activity: prices fell 36% and industrial production roughly 50% over the course of 1929-1933 (p.303). During the same time frame banking panics were quite frequent (Friedman and Schwartz, [19], p.308-328). Also Fisher [18], Calomiris [6], Calomiris and Mason [8], and Warren and Pearson [31] argue that the fall in the price level significantly reduced the value of firms and banks' assets relative to the value of their liabilities, forcing them to fail.

Furthermore, Wicker [33] offers evidence that currency usage replaced checks during the banking failures of the Great Depression[43], and, for the same time period, Richardson [25] documents the critical role played by payment system's disruptions in the propagation of banking panics[44] especially through the failure of correspondent banks[45].

## A.2  Japan during the 1990s

In Japan during the 1990s, often referred to as the *Lost Decade*, prices fell considerably (1.5% every year since mid 1990s until 2002) and real activity grew on average only 1% every year during the period 1991-2002[46]: the existence of a deposit insurance agency prevented bank runs but banking difficulties and banking failures were widespread. Figure 5 shows that at the same time as prices started falling, between 1998 and 2003, financial assistance granted by the Japan Deposit Insurance Corporation to banks increased dramatically going from nearly zero in 1997 to 5 trillions ¥ in 2000, then remaining substantially high around 2 trillions ¥ until 2002 while prices kept falling until 2003[47].

## A.3  US: 2007-2010

The United States between 2007 and 2010 experienced very low inflation which turned into deflation in the second half of 2008, accompanied by several hundreds of banking failures[48]

---

[43] [33], pg. 45

[44] See pg. 644

[45] Correspondent banks were banks that cleared checks for other banks (respondents).

[46] Baba et al., [1]

[47] Sources: CPI: International Financial Statistics, Consumer Prices; Grants by JDIC: Deposit Insurance Corporation of Japan, DICJ's Activities, Financial Assistance.

[48] See Failed Financial Institutions, FDIC public website

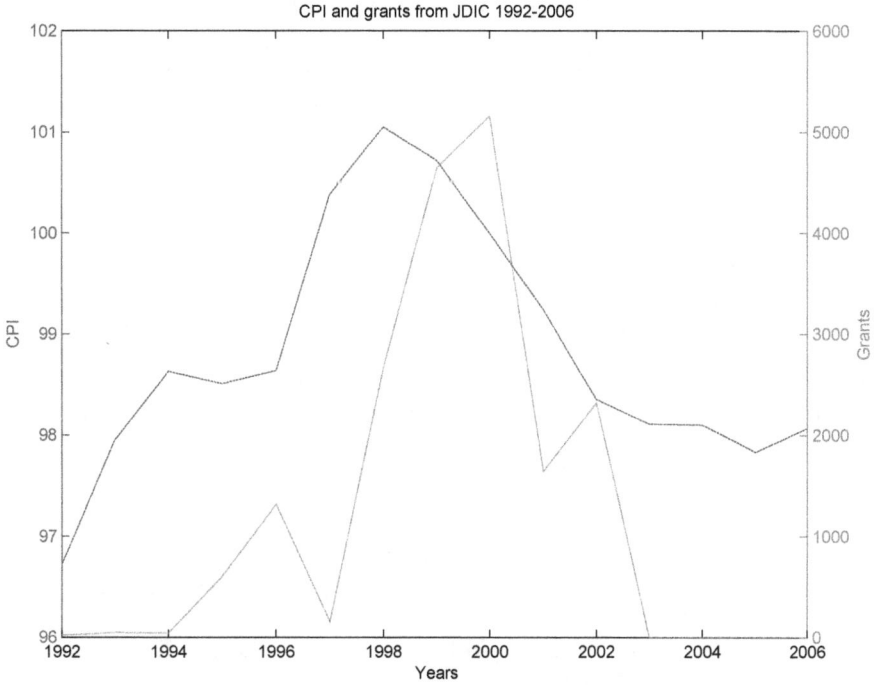

FIGURE 5: Cases of Financial Assistance in Japan, ¥ billions

and bankruptcies of some large investment banks[49]. Figure 6 shows that the timing of bankruptcies by the largest institutions and price declines was the same: between August and December 2008 prices kept falling and financial institutions failing.

Figure 6 also shows that as prices started falling, cash held by the public jumped from $770 billions in August 2008 to $850 billions by the first quarter of 2009[50]. Therefore failures of banks and other financial institutions were accompanied by declines in prices and an increase in cash holdings in households' portfolios.

---

[49]Bear Stearns, March $14^{th}$2008 and Merrill Lynch, Lehman Brothers, Washington Mutual between September and October 2008.

[50]Sources: CPI: Bureau of Labor Statistics, series id: SUUR0000SA0; cash held by the public: Federal Reserve Board of Governors, Federal Reserve Statistical Release, Historical Data, Table 4: Components of M1, Currency (http://www.federalreserve.gov/releases/h6/hist/h6hist4.txt)

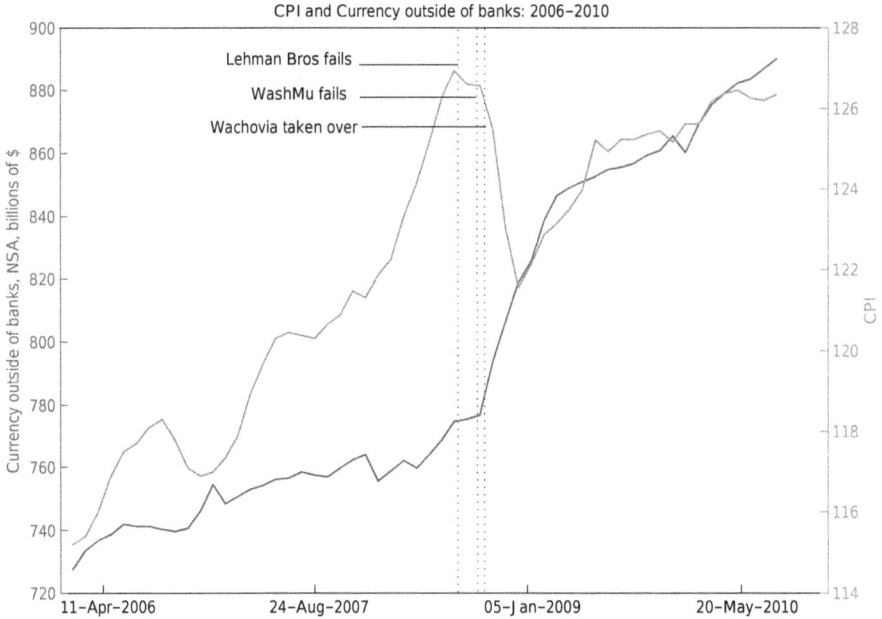

FIGURE 6: CPI and cash held by the public in the US, $ billions

# B Appendix

A version of the paper with a more detailed appendix and extensive proofs can be found at http://sites.google.com/site/carapellaf/research

## B.1 Proof of Proposition 1

For the no default equilibrium, assumptions 1-3 guarantee that a solution to households' problem (1) exists and is interior and market clearing prices are strictly positive, denoted $p^{nd}$. Given such allocation and prices, assumption 2 guarantees that banks' assets exceed liabilities, $p^{nd}f > R$, and assumption 8 guarantees that no strategic default occurs.

For the default equilibrium, assumption 1 guarantees that the allocation that solves households' problem (1) exists and is interior and prices are strictly positive, denoted $p^d$. Given such allocation and prices, banks default because assumption 2 implies $p^d f > R$.

Also, assumption 3 guarantees that $p^{nd} > p^d$.

A sufficient condition for households' welfare to be higher in no default[51] is $\left(\frac{1}{2}\right)^2 <$

---

[51]In a static environment it is not obvious that the equilibrium with no default yields higher utility to households because the planting technology is independent of banks' default and because the claims of

$\left(\frac{rA}{[r(1+r)A-R(2r-1)]}\sqrt{r(1+r)}\left(\frac{3r-2}{2r-1}\right)^{\frac{1}{2}}\right)^2$ which is satisfied by assumption 2.

## B.2  Proof of Proposition 2

The equilibrium is constructed by defining strategies for banks and households as follows: banks default if the sunspot hits and do not default otherwise. Households do not deposit in bank $j$ if bank $j$ defaults and deposit $D^{nd}$ to solve households' problem (10) otherwise.

Let $x_t^s = (c_{1t}^s, c_{2t}^s, M_t^s, D_t^s, A_{t+1}^s)$ denote the allocation that solves the households' problem with the constructed strategies, where $s = d, nd$ according to whether banks default or not.

When the sunspot hits, the solution to the households' problem is such that $c_1^d = c_2^d = \frac{\overline{M}}{2p^d}$ since the relevant cash in advance constraint is (13). Then the resource constraint: $f(\frac{D^{nd}}{p^{nd}}, L) + \frac{\overline{M}}{p^d} = y + f(\frac{D^{nd}}{p^{nd}}, L)$, implies $p^d = \frac{\overline{M}}{y}$.

Before the sunspot hits, assumption 4 guarantees that a solution to the households' problem exists and is interior. Given allocation $x^{nd}$ and prices $p^{nd}$, assumption 6 guarantees that banks' net assets are strictly positive, $f(i^{nd}, L) - \frac{R^{nd}D^{nd}}{p^{nd}} = (i^{nd})^\alpha L^{1-\alpha}(1 - \frac{\alpha}{\pi}) > 0$, and assumption 8 guarantees that the real value of paying depositors back is smaller than the present discounted value of future profits: $\frac{R^{nd}D^{nd}}{p^{nd}} < \gamma w^{j,nd}$. Therefore at prices $p^{nd}$ banks are solvent and no strategic default occurs.

At prices $p^d$ a bank $j$ defaults if and only if $f(i^{nd}, L) - \frac{R^{nd}D^{nd}}{p^d} = (i^{nd})^\alpha L^{1-\alpha}(1 - \frac{\alpha}{\pi}\frac{p^{nd}}{p^d}) < 0$ that is to say if and only if $\frac{p^d}{p^{nd}} < \frac{\alpha}{\pi}$, which is satisfied by assumption 5.

Assumptions 4-5 then imply that $p^{nd} > p^d$.

---

coconut that households have on banks are exogenous. In the default equilibrium households' utility loss is caused by financial disintermediation (no payment instruments alternative to cash) and by the loss of wealth ($R$ units of coconut). However there is a utility gain caused by equalizing the marginal rate of substitution between cash and credit goods with the marginal rate of transformation because the relevant cash-in-advance constraint binds on both goods. Therefore, for the no default equilibrium to yield higher utility to households, it must be the case that the loss is large enough.

In a dynamic environment, because households' claims on banks are linked to the deposit decision, then the allocation of consumption and asset holdings that solves the households' problem in default, say $x^d$, is still in households' constraint set in no default. Therefore if a solution to the households' problem in no default, say $x^{nd}$, is different from $x^d$, it must be the case that households' utility is higher in no default.

## B.3  Proof of Proposition 3

Consider bank $j$ default decision problem at time $\widehat{t}$ with existing deposits $D^{nd} > 0$[52]. with active monetary policy, the stock of money supply conditional on history $h_1^{\widehat{t}} = (h^{\widehat{t}-1}, \theta_{\widehat{t}} = 1, ((\delta(j') = 1)_{j' \in [0,1] \setminus j}, \delta(j) = 0))$ is $\overline{M}'(h_1^{\widehat{t}}) = \overline{M} + T_{\widehat{t}}(h^{\widehat{t}-1}) = p^{nd}y$. Assumption 6 then implies that bank $j$ is solvent and its payoffs, conditional on banks $j' \in [0,1] \setminus \{j\}$ actions, are shown in Figure 7, where $p^{(\delta(j),\delta(j'))}$ denotes the resulting equilibrium price if bank $k = j, j'$'s default decision is $\delta(k)$ so that $p^{(0,1)} = p^d$ and $p^{(0,0)} = p^{nd}$. Then assumption 8 implies that default is a strictly dominated strategy for bank $j$.

banks  $j'$

|  | $\delta(j') = 1$ | $\delta(j') = 0$ |
|---|---|---|
| $\delta(j) = 1$ | $f$ | $f$ |
| $\delta(j) = 0$ | $f - \dfrac{R^{nd}D^{nd}}{p^{(0,1)}} + \gamma w^j$ | $f - \dfrac{R^{nd}D^{nd}}{p^{(0,0)}} + \gamma w^j$ |

bank  $j$  (row label)

FIGURE 7: Bank $j$ payoffs conditional on banks $-j$ actions.

## B.4  Proof of Proposition 4

### Proof of Proposition 4. 1

**Claim 1** *Without deposit insurance investing in the safe technology is an equilibrium.*

**Proof** Consider bank $j$ investment decision problem at time $\widehat{t}$ with existing deposits $D^{nd}$. Let a measure one of banks invest in the safe technology. It is sufficient to rule out one shot deviations by a single bank $j$, even at a node following a deviation.

At time $t$, bank $j$'s payoffs in each state of the world, conditional on households' and banks' strategies, are shown in Table B.1. When $\widehat{r} = \underline{r} < 0$ bank $j$ must default since it doesn't have enough assets to pay its liabilities. When $\widehat{r} = \overline{r}$, at prices $p^{nd}$ assumptions 6 and 8 respectively imply that bank $j$ is solvent and chooses not to strategically default. When $\widehat{r} = \overline{r}$, at prices are $p^d$, assumption 9 provides a sufficient condition for bank $j$ to default. At time $\widehat{t}$, if bank $j$ invests in $\widehat{f}$, then it defaults in more states of the world than

---

[52]If existing deposits are zero, $D^{nd} = 0$, then bank $j$ has no liabilities, so it does not default.

TABLE B.1: No deposit insurance: Bank $j$'s payoffs if other banks invest in $f$

| $\hat{r}$ | Prices | Net assets | No default | Default |
|---|---|---|---|---|
| $\underline{r}$ | $p^{nd}$ | $\underline{r}(\frac{D^{nd}}{p^{nd}})^\alpha L^{1-\alpha} - \frac{R^{nd}D^{nd}}{p^{nd}} < 0$ | | $0$ |
| $\underline{r}$ | $p^d$ | $\underline{r}(\frac{D^{nd}}{p^{nd}})^\alpha L^{1-\alpha} - \frac{R^{nd}D^{nd}}{p^d} < 0$ | | $0$ |
| $\bar{r}$ | $p^{nd}$ | $\bar{r}(\frac{D^{nd}}{p^{nd}})^\alpha L^{1-\alpha} - \frac{R^{nd}D^{nd}}{p^{nd}} > 0$ | $\bar{r}(\frac{D^{nd}}{p^{nd}})^\alpha L^{1-\alpha} - \frac{R^{nd}D^{nd}}{p^{nd}} + \gamma w^j$ | $\bar{r}(\frac{D^{nd}}{p^{nd}})^\alpha L^{1-\alpha}$ |
| $\bar{r}$ | $p^d$ | $\bar{r}(\frac{D^{nd}}{p^{nd}})^\alpha L^{1-\alpha} - \frac{R^{nd}D^{nd}}{p^d} < 0$ | $\bar{r}(\frac{D^{nd}}{p^{nd}})^\alpha L^{1-\alpha} - \frac{R^{nd}D^{nd}}{p^d} + \gamma w^j$ | $\bar{r}(\frac{D^{nd}}{p^{nd}})^\alpha L^{1-\alpha}$ |

banks that invest in the safe technology $f$. Therefore households do not deposit in bank $j$ and investing in the risky technology is a strictly dominated strategy.[53].

At a node following a deviation, bank $j$ has no liabilities because households do not deposit at banks that invest in $\hat{f}$, and it also has no assets because if it deviated in the previous period bank $j$ had no deposits and no resources to finance investment into production. Therefore, the relevant payoffs are as in table B.1 and assumptions 6 and 8 guaranteed that also at a node following a previous deviation, investing in the risky technology $\hat{f}$ is a strictly dominated strategy[54]. ∎

---

[53]The payoffs to bank $j$ at time $t$ from deviating and playing the constructed strategy, are respectively:

$$W_t^j(h^{t-1}, \theta_t = 0, \delta_t(j) = 0, \hat{f}) = f(i_{t-1,L}) - \frac{R^{nd}D^{nd}}{p^{nd}} + \gamma[0 + \Pr(nd)\gamma w_{t+2}^j(h_1^{t+1})]$$

$$W_t^j(h^{t-1}, \theta_t = 0, \delta_t(j) = 0, f) = f(i_{t-1,L}) - \frac{R^{nd}D^{nd}}{p^{nd}} + \gamma[f(i_{t-1,L}) - \Pr(nd)\frac{R^{nd}D^{nd}}{p^{nd}} + \Pr(nd)\gamma w_{t+2}^j(h_1^{t+1})]$$

where the current payoff $f(i_{t-1,L}) - \frac{R^{nd}D^{nd}}{p^{nd}}$ the continuation value $w_{t+2}^j(h_1^{t+1})$ is the same under both strategies because investing in $\hat{f}$ is a one shot deviation. Assumption 6 implies $W_t^j(h^t, \theta_t = 0, \delta_t(j) = 0, f) > W_t^j(h^t, \theta_t = 0, \delta_t(j) = 0, \hat{f})$ then bank $j$ invests in $f$.

[54]The payoffs to bank $j$ from from deviating and playing the constructed strategy at a node following a previous deviation are respectively:

$$W_{t+1}^j(h^t, \theta_{t+1} = 0, \delta_{t+1}(j) = 0, \hat{f}) = 0 + \gamma[0 + \Pr(nd)\gamma w_{t+2}^j(h_1^{t+1})]$$

$$W_{t+1}^j(h^t, \theta_{t+1} = 0, \delta_{t+1}(j) = 0, f) = 0 + \gamma[f(i_{t-1,L}) - \Pr(nd)\frac{R^{nd}D^{nd}}{p^{nd}} + \Pr(nd)\gamma w_{t+2}^j(h_1^{t+1})]$$

**Claim 2** *Without deposit insurance investing in the risky technology is not an equilibrium.*

**Proof** Suppose there exists an equilibrium where banks invest in the risky technology. It is easy to construct a profitable deviation for bank $j$ as follows: invest in the safe technology $f$ today, offer households the same deposit contract as other banks investing in $\widehat{f}$ offer, and follow the same strategy played by other banks from tomorrow on. The interest rate on deposit contracts offered by banks investing in $\widehat{f}$ is $R_s = \frac{p_{s+1}}{p_s} \frac{E(\widehat{r})}{q\pi} \alpha (\frac{D_s}{p_s})^{\alpha-1} L^{1-\alpha}$ and assumption 10 guarantees that it is always feasible for bank $j$ to offer the same contract[55]. Then the expected continuation payoff to bank $j$ is the same as the continuation payoff to every bank investing in $\widehat{f}$. The current payoff from investing in $f$, however, is strictly larger because $\widehat{f}$ is a mean reducing spread of $f$. Therefore investing in $f$ is a profitable deviation for bank $j$. ∎

## Proof of Proposition 4. 2

**Proof** If a measure one of banks does not default, Proposition 2 implies that the unique best response for an individual bank is not to default as well.

If the sunspot hits at time $\widehat{t}$ and a measure one of banks defaults then banks' assets are seized by the deposit insurer, and their real value is $f(i^{nd}, L) = r(i^{nd})^{\alpha} L^{1-\alpha}$. The real value of banks' liabilities to the insurer is $\frac{R^{nd} D^{nd}}{p_{\widehat{t}}}$ where $p_{\widehat{t}}$ is the price level at time $\widehat{t}$. Since real resources exceed the real value of liabilities at the price level anticipated in the deposit contract, then with deposit insurance bank-issued payment instruments are still viable, and the solution to the households' problem is the same as in no default: $(c_1^{nd}, c_2^{nd}, D^{nd}, M^{nd}, i^{nd})$ and the resulting equilibrium price is $p_{\widehat{t}} = p^{nd}$. Assumptions 6, 8 then guarantee that banks' net assets are strictly positive and that the payoff from strategic default is smaller than the payoff from being in business. Therefore the unique best response for an individual bank is not to default. ∎

## Proof of Proposition 4. 3

---

Assumption 6 implies $W_{t+1}^{j}(h^t, \theta_{t+1} = 0, \delta_{t+1}(j) = 0, f) > W_{t+1}^{j}(h^t, \theta_{t+1} = 0, \delta_{t+1}(j) = 0, \widehat{f})$.

[55] Its assets net of liabilities would be:

$$i_s^{\alpha} L^{1-\alpha} - \frac{p_{s+1}}{p_s} \frac{E(\widehat{r})}{q\pi} \alpha (\frac{D_s}{p_s})^{\alpha-1} L^{1-\alpha} \frac{D_s}{p_s} = (\frac{D_s}{p_s})^{\alpha} L^{1-\alpha} - \frac{p_{s+1}}{p_s} \frac{E(\widehat{r})}{q\pi} \alpha (\frac{D_s}{p_s})^{\alpha-1} L^{1-\alpha} \frac{D_s}{p_s}$$

$$= (1 - \frac{E(\widehat{r})\alpha}{q\pi})(\frac{D_s}{p_s})^{\alpha} L^{1-\alpha} > 0$$

**Claim 3** *Without strict regulations investing in the risky technology is an equilibrium.*

**Proof** If every bank $j' \in [0,1] \setminus j$ invests in $\widehat{f}$ then bank $j$'s payoffs in every state of the world according to its choice of technology and default are shown in Table B.2, where the interest rate on existing deposits is the same regardless of whether banks choose $\widehat{f}$ or $f$ because by construction deposit insurance is established after households' deposit decision and before banks' investment decision, so the deposit contract has already been signed.

Also, the continuation value $w^j$ associated with investing in $\widehat{f}$ is the same as the one associated with $f$, given that deposit insurance is a one time policy experiment. Therefore $\forall t > \widehat{t}$ banks invest in the safe technology by Proposition 4.1, regardless of the technology they choose at time $\widehat{t}$, and households' choice of deposits is $D^{nd}$.

TABLE B.2: Deposit insurance, no regulations: Bank $j$'s payoffs if other banks invest in $\widehat{f}$

| | $\widehat{r}$ | Prices | Net assets | No default | Default |
|---|---|---|---|---|---|
| $\widehat{f}$ | $\underline{r}$ | $p^d$ | $\underline{r}(\frac{D^{nd}}{p^{nd}})^\alpha L^{1-\alpha} - \frac{R^{nd}D^{nd}}{p^d} < 0$ | | 0 |
| | $\overline{r}$ | $p^{nd}$ | $\overline{r}(\frac{D^{nd}}{p^{nd}})^\alpha L^{1-\alpha} - \frac{R^{nd}D^{nd}}{p^{nd}} > 0$ | $\overline{r}(\frac{D^{nd}}{p^{nd}})^\alpha L^{1-\alpha} - \frac{R^{nd}D^{nd}}{p^{nd}} + \gamma w^j.$ | 0 |
| $f$ | $\underline{r}$ | $p^d$ | $(\frac{D^{nd}}{p^{nd}})^\alpha L^{1-\alpha} - \frac{R^{nd}D^{nd}}{p^d} < 0$ | | 0 |
| | $\overline{r}$ | $p^{nd}$ | $(\frac{D^{nd}}{p^{nd}})^\alpha L^{1-\alpha} - \frac{RD^{nd}}{p^{nd}} > 0$ | $(\frac{D^{nd}}{p^{nd}})^\alpha L^{1-\alpha} - \frac{RD^{nd}}{p^{nd}} + \gamma w^j$ | 0 |

When $\widehat{r} = \underline{r} < 0$, if bank $j$ invested in $\widehat{f}$, then it must default because the return on its assets is negative and it cannot pay its liabilities. Also, equilibrium prices are $p^d$, because every bank $j'$ does not have enough real resources to cover the real value of its liabilities even at the price level anticipated in the deposit contract. Therefore the deposit insurer cannot make payment instruments issued by banks still viable and at prices $p^d$ bank $j$ must default even if it invested in $f$ because by assumptions 5 its liabilities exceed its assets.

When $\widehat{r} = \overline{r} > 1$, if bank $j$ invested in $f$, then assumptions 6 and 8 guarantee that it does not default[56]. Similarly, if bank $j$ invested in $\widehat{f}$, then under assumptions 6 and 8 it does not default because $\overline{r} > 1$.

Assumption 11 then guarantees that bank $j$'s best response is to invest in $\widehat{f}$ if and only if $q[\overline{r}i_{t-1}^\alpha L^{1-\alpha} - \frac{R_{t-1}D_{t-1}}{p_t} + \gamma w_{t+1}^j] > [i_{t-1}^\alpha L^{1-\alpha} - \frac{R_{t-1}D_{t-1}}{p_t} + \gamma w_{t+1}^j]$, which can be rewritten

---

[56]By assumptions 6 banks' assets are strictly positive and by assumption 8 strategic default is not a best response.

as:

$$q[\bar{r} - \frac{\alpha}{\pi} + \frac{\gamma(1-\alpha)}{(1-\gamma\pi)}] \quad > \quad [1 - \frac{\alpha}{\pi} + \frac{\gamma(1-\alpha)}{(1-\gamma\pi)}] \tag{19}$$

Assumption 11 guarantees that (19) is satisfied. ∎

**Claim 4** *Without strict regulations investing in the safe technology is not an equilibrium.*

**Proof** If every bank $j' \in [0,1] \setminus j$ invests in $f$ then bank $j$'s payoffs in every state of the world according to its choice of technology and default are shown in Table B.3.

TABLE B.3: Deposit insurance, no regulations: Bank $j$'s payoffs if other banks invest in $f$

| | $\widehat{r}$ | Prices | Net assets | No default | Default |
|---|---|---|---|---|---|
| $\widehat{f}$ | $\underline{r}$ | $p^{nd}$ | $\underline{r}(\frac{D^{nd}}{p^{nd}})^\alpha L^{1-\alpha} - \frac{R^{nd}D^{nd}}{p^d} < 0$ | | 0 |
| | $\bar{r}$ | $p^{nd}$ | $\bar{r}(\frac{D^{nd}}{p^{nd}})^\alpha L^{1-\alpha} - \frac{R^{nd}D^{nd}}{p^{nd}} > 0$ | $\bar{r}(\frac{D^{nd}}{p^{nd}})^\alpha L^{1-\alpha} - \frac{R^{nd}D^{nd}}{p^{nd}} + \gamma w^j$ | 0 |
| $f$ | | $p^{nd}$ | $(\frac{D^{nd}}{p^{nd}})^\alpha L^{1-\alpha} - \frac{RD^{nd}}{p^{nd}} > 0$ | $(\frac{D^{nd}}{p^{nd}})^\alpha L^{1-\alpha} - \frac{RD^{nd}}{p^{nd}} + \gamma w^j$ | 0 |

Because banks invest in the safe technology, then they always have enough real resources to cover the real value of their liabilities at the price level that was anticipated in the deposit contract. Therefore, with deposit insurance their liabilities are always a viable means of payment, and, as a consequence, equilibrium prices are $p^{nd}$.

When $\widehat{r} = \underline{r} < 0$, if bank $j$ invested in $\widehat{f}$ then it must default, if it invested in $f$ then assumptions 6 and 8 imply that it does not default. When $\widehat{r} = \bar{r} > 1$, if bank $j$ invested in $\widehat{f}$ then assumptions 6, 8 imply that it does not default because $\bar{r} > 1$ . Assumption 11 then guarantees that bank $j$'s best response is to choose $\widehat{f}$. ∎

# C   Appendix

## C.1   Restrictions on banks' discount factor

In the equilibrium constructed in proposition 2, at the beginning of period $t$, before the sunspot hits, banks' expected profits are:

$$w_t^j(h_1^t, i_{t-1}, D_{t-1}^b) = \max_{\{x_t^k, s_t^k, D_t^{b,k}, i_t^k\}} \{\pi[x_t^{nd} + \gamma w_{t+1}^j(h_1^{t+1}, i_t^{nd}, D_t^{b,nd})] + \tag{20}$$

$$+ (1-\pi)[x_t^d + \gamma w_{t+1}^{d,j}(h_1^{t+1}, i_t^d, D_t^{b,d})]\}$$

$$s.t. \qquad x_t^{nd} + s_t^{nd} \leq f(i_{t-1}, L) - \frac{R_{t-1} D_{t-1}}{p_t} \qquad (21)$$

$$x_t^{d} + s_t^{d} \leq f(i_{t-1}, L) \qquad (22)$$

$$p_t i_t^{nd} \leq D_t^{b,nd} + p_t s_t^{nd} \qquad (23)$$

$$p_t i_t^{d} \leq D_t^{b,d} + p_t s_t^{d} \qquad (24)$$

where $x_t^k, k = d, nd$ denotes time $t$ consumption of bank $j$ in default and no default; similarly $s_t^k$ denotes savings, $i_t^k$ investment into the productive technology and $D_t^{b,k}$ deposits offered[57]. Under assumption 7 a solution to problem (20) is such that $s_t^{nd} = 0$.

# D   Appendix

## D.1   Banks and Firms

This appendix provides a modified version of the model of section 2 to allow for banks to make nominal loans to firms rather than owning productive projects directly, and for banks to strategically default. Even if this appendix deals only with the one period model, the same characterization applies to the dynamic model of section 3 for the *involuntary* defaults.

None of the results in the paper change qualitatively: different partitions of the state space would have to be assumed in propositions 1-4 and every result goes through. Therefore, in the main body of the paper a simpler model where banks and firms are consolidated has been privileged.

Consider an economy populated by three types of agents: households, banks and firms. They are identical within their type, there is a continuum $[0, 1]$ of each and all live for one period. Consumption goods are as in section 2, as well as preferences and endowments for households and banks: the only difference for banks is that they are endowed with labor, $l$, and a technology that uses labor to produce an input good $z$ (this can be interpreted as a loan). Let $z^b$ denote the output of good $z$ produced by banks, then $z^b = F(l)$. As in section 2, they are endowed with a technology that allows them to plant coconut and which returns $r$ per unit of coconut planted: households deposit coconut at banks, $D$ which gives rise to an obligation for banks to pay $R$ units of coconut to households at the end of the period.

---

[57]Because this paper does not focus on coordination failures on the side of depositors, banks' ability to pay households for deposits they made in the previous period, is independent of deposits households make in the current period. This can be seen from (21) and (22) where banks do not have resources available from current period deposits ($D_t^{b,k}$) to pay for their obligations ($R_{t-1} D_{t-1}$).

Firms' preferences are linear in both the consumption of cash and credit goods: $V^f(c_1^f, c_2^f) = c_1^f + c_2^f$ . Firms are endowed with a technology $f(z)$ that uses the input good to produce either cash or credit goods: let $z^f$ denote the input of good $z$ firms choose to invest into production.

There is free entry into banking and there is a competitive market to trade good $z$ that opens at the beginning of the period, before the market for cash and credit goods opens, where firms buy good $z$ and banks sell good $z$ at price $p_z$. Then the goods' market opens, where firms can sell the output of cash and credit goods from their productive technology at price $p$: they are paid wither with coconut or with bank-issued liabilities or both (as in section 2).

Differently from section 2, at the end of the period firms have to settle with banks for their purchases of good $z$ made at the beginning of the period (firms have to pay back the loan).

Then on this market so that their decision problems, respectively, are:

# References

[1] N. Baba, S. Nishioka, N. Oda, M. Shirakawa, K. Ueda, and H. Ugai. Japan's deflation problems in the financial system and monetary policy. *BIS working paper*, No. 274, March 2007.

[2] B. Bernanke. Nonmonetary effects of the financial crisis in the propagation of the great depression. *The American Economic Review*, 73 No. 3:257–276, June 1983.

[3] B. Bernanke and M. Gertler. Financial fragility and economic performance. *NBER working papers series*, No. 2318, July 1987.

[4] B. Bernanke and M. Gertler. Agency costs, net worth and business fluctuations. *The American Economic Review*, 79 No. 1:14–31, March 1989.

[5] B. Bernanke, M. Gertler, and S. Gilchrist. The financial accelerator and the flight to quality. *The Review of Economics and Statistics*, 78 No. 1:1–15, February 1996.

[6] C. Calomiris. Banking failures in theory and history: The great depression and other "contagious" events. *NBER Working Paper*, N. 13597, November 2007.

[7] C. Calomiris and G. Gorton. The origins of banking panics. In *Hubbard,R.Glenn, Financial Markets and Financial Crises*, pages 109–173. The University of Chicago Press, 1991.

[8] C. Calomiris and J. R. Mason. Causes of us bank distress during the depression. *NBER Working Paper*, N. 7919, September 2000.

[9] C. Calomiris and E. N. White. The origins of federal deposit insurance. In *Goldin, Claudia and Gary D. Libecap, The Regulated Economy*, pages 145–188. The University of Chicago Press, 1994.

[10] C. T. Carlstrom and T. Fuerst. Agency costs, net worth and business fluctuations: A computable general equilibrium analysis. *The American Economic Review*, 87 No. 5, 1997.

[11] V. V. Chari. Banking without deposit insurance or bank panics: Lessons from a model of the u.s. national banking system. *Federal Reserve Bank of Minneapolis, Quarterly Review*, 13 No. 3, Summer 1989.

[12] V. V. Chari, L. Christiano, and M. Eichenbaum. Inside money, outside money, and short-term interest rates. *Journal of Money, Credit and Banking*, 27 No. 4 Part 2:1354–1386, November 1995.

[13] V. V. Chari and R. Jagannathan. Banking panics, information, and rational expectations equilibrium. *Journal of Finance*, 13 No. 3 Part 2:749–761, July 1988.

[14] H. L. Cole and L. E. Ohanian. Deflation and the international great depression: A productivity puzzle. *Federal Reserve Bank of Minneapolis Research Department Staff Report*, February 2005.

[15] D. Diamond and P. Dybvig. Bank runs, deposit insurance and liquidity. *Journal of Political Economy*, 91:401–19, June 1983.

[16] D. Diamond and R. Rajan. Money in a theory of banking. *American Economic Review*, 96:30–53, 1 2006.

[17] H. Ennis and T. Keister. Commitment and equilibrium bank runs. *Federal Reserve Bank of New York Staff Report*, N. 274, March 2007.

[18] I. Fisher. The debt-deflation theory of the great depression. *Econometrica*, 1 No. 4:337–357, October 1933.

[19] M. Friedman and A. J. Schwartz. *A Monetary History of the United States, 1967-1960*. Princeton University Press, 1963.

[20] G. Gorton. *Banking Panics and Business Cycles*. Oxford Economic Papers, 40, 1988.

[21] E. J. Green and P. Lin. Implementing efficient allocations in a model of financial inter-mediation. *Federal Reserve Bank of Minneapolis Research Department Staff Report*, 109:1–23, 2003.

[22] R. E. Lucas and N. L. Stokey. Optimal fiscal and monetary policy in an economy without capital. *Journal of Monetary Economics*, N.12:55–93, 1983.

[23] R. E. Lucas and N. L. Stokey. Money and interest in a cash-in-advance economy. *Econometrica*, 55, N.3:491–513, May 1987.

[24] A. Martin. Liquidity provision vs deposit insurance: preventing bank panics without moral hazard. *Economic Theory*, 28:197–211, 2006.

[25] G. Richardson. The check is in the mail: correspondent clearing and the collapse of the banking system, 1930 to 1933. *The Journal of Economic History*, 67 N. 3:643–671, September 2007.

[26] O. Sprague. *History of Crises Under the National Banking System*. Report by the National Monetary Commission to the U.S. Senate. 61st Cong., 2nd sess., S. Doc. 538, Government Printing Office, Washington, D.C, 1910.

[27] C. Warburton. Monetary expansion and the inflationary gap. *American Economic Review*, 34:303–327, 2 Part 1 1944.

[28] C. Warburton. Monetary theory, full production and the great depression. *Econometrica*, 13 N. 2:114–128, 1945.

[29] C. Warburton. Quantity and frequency of use of money in the united states, 1919-45. *The Journal of Political Economy*, 54 N.5:436–450, 1945.

[30] C. Warburton. The volume of money and the price level between the world wars. *The Journal of Political Economy*, 53 N. 2:150–163, 1945.

[31] G. F. Warren and F. A. Pearson. *Prices*. New York: John Wiley, 1933.

[32] E. N. White. The legacy of deposit insurance. In *Bordo, Michael D., Claudia Goldin and Eugene White, The Defining Moment*, pages 87–124. The University of Chicago Press, 1998.

[33] E. Wicker. *The Banking Panics of the Great Depression*. Cambridge University Press, 1996.